barbecue

barbecue

This edition published in 2009

Love Food ® is an imprint of Parragon Books Ltd

Parragon
Queen Street House
4 Queen Street
Bath BA1 1HE, UK

Cover design by Talking Design
Photography by Günter Beer
Home economy by Stevan Paul

ISBN 978-1-4075-6966-6

Printed in China

Notes for the reader
• This book uses both metric and imperial measurements. Follow the same units of measurement throughout; do not mix metric and imperial. All spoon measurements are level: teaspoons are assumed to be 5 ml, and tablespoons are assumed to be 15 ml. Unless otherwise stated, milk is assumed to be full fat, eggs and individual vegetables are medium, and pepper is freshly ground black pepper.
• The times given are an approximate guide only. Preparation times differ according to the techniques used by different people and the cooking times may also vary from those given. Optional ingredients, variations or serving suggestions have not been included in the calculations.
• Recipes using raw or very lightly cooked eggs should be avoided by infants, the elderly, pregnant women, convalescents and anyone suffering from an illness. Pregnant and breastfeeding women are advised to avoid eating peanuts and peanut products. Sufferers from nut allergies should be aware that some of the ready-made ingredients used in the recipes in this book may contain nuts. Always check the packaging before use.

Contents

6   Introduction

8   Meat & Poultry

34 Fish & Seafood

54 Vegetarian & Accompaniments

78 Desserts & Treats

96 Index

Introduction

If you mention summer cooking and entertaining to anyone, their first thought would have to be – barbecue! After the doom and gloom of cold wet winter days, the arrival of summer means a whole new way of cooking and eating. Barbecued food is easy to prepare, quick to cook and the ideal sunshine food, and appeals to kids and adults alike. The allure of outdoor eating is not difficult to pinpoint – food tastes better in the fresh air and the delicious cooking smells only add to the hunger levels, which means food cooked outdoors is always well received! The recipes in this delightful collection will ensure your barbecue is a complete success, from stunning side dishes to marvellous mains.

One of the first things to consider when deciding to hold a barbecue is whether you want to use gas or charcoal for heat. This is more of a lifestyle choice. If you are convinced that food cooked over hot charcoal has the best flavour and take pride in getting the fire started, then charcoal is for you. Alternatively, if you want the perfect fire at the touch of a button and to be able to control the temperature, then a gas barbecue is the ideal choice.

If you opt for a charcoal barbecue, there are a few general rules you can follow to ensure success. Firstly, keep the charcoal briquettes dry, preferably in an airtight container, to help the charcoal light faster. Place the briquettes in a pyramid in the centre of the grill. If you are using barbecue lighter fluid, douse this evenly over the briquettes and allow to soak in for a few minutes. If you are using barbecue fire lighters, poke these between the briquettes about a third of the way up the pyramid. Using long kitchen matches, either light the doused briquettes or the

fire lighters. The charcoal will take about 30 minutes to get hot. Once the briquettes start to get hot, they will glow a red to orange colour, then gradually turn to a whitish grey. It is the white ash over the coals that tell you they are really hot. Now you can spread them out evenly over the bottom of the barbecue. Do not worry if some of the coals from the centre of the pyramid are still orange – just give them a few more minutes to turn grey too. Place the cooking metal grill over the top. It is a good idea to wait a few more minutes before adding the food, in order to allow the grill to heat up really well.

Barbecue food should be kept simple and fuss-free – without compromising on taste. The chapters in this book will cater for all tastes and will ensure your barbecue is a complete success. 'Meat & Poultry' contains all the classics no barbecue would be complete without, including a few new ideas – try the Brandy Steaks for a twist on the usual barbecued steaks. 'Fish & Seafood' provides mouthwatering ideas for delicious fish dishes, such as the Orange & Lemon Peppered Monkfish. Vegetarians are often forgotten about at barbecues or have to make do with a salad – try turning to the 'Vegetarian & Accompaniments' chapter for lots of exciting ideas that will please vegetarians and meat-lovers alike, such as the Courgette & Cheese Parcels. And to finish, 'Desserts & Treats' will provide plenty of sweet treats, such as the Toffee Fruit Kebabs. There is also a recipe for Sangria included – a non-alcoholic version, to avoid any barbecue mishaps!

So get the barbecue going and let this book guide you through the best barbecue food ever!

Meat & Poultry

serves 4

4 beef steaks

4 tbsp brandy or whisky

2 tbsp soy sauce

1 tbsp dark muscovado sugar

pepper

tomato slices

fresh flat-leaf parsley sprigs,
to garnish

garlic bread, to serve

brandy steaks

Make a few cuts in the edge of the fat on each steak. This will
stop the meat curling as it cooks. Place the meat in a shallow,
non-metallic dish.

Mix the brandy, soy sauce, sugar and pepper to taste together in
a small bowl, stirring until the sugar dissolves. Pour the mixture
over the steak. Cover with clingfilm and leave to marinate in the
refrigerator for at least 2 hours.

Preheat the barbecue. Cook the meat over hot coals, searing
the meat over the hottest part of the barbecue for 2 minutes
on each side.

Move the meat to an area with slightly less intense heat and
cook for a further 4–10 minutes on each side, depending on
how well done you like your steaks. To test if the meat is cooked,
insert the point of a sharp knife into the meat – the juices will
run from red when the meat is still rare, to clear as it becomes
well cooked.

Lightly barbecue the tomato slices for 1–2 minutes. Transfer the
meat and the tomatoes to serving plates. Garnish with fresh
parsley sprigs and serve with garlic bread.

serves 4

2 tbsp sunflower oil,
plus extra for oiling

finely grated rind of 1 lime

1 tbsp lime juice

2 garlic cloves, crushed

1/4 tsp ground coriander

1/4 tsp ground cumin

pinch of sugar

salt and pepper

1 piece of rump steak, about
675 g/1 lb 8 oz and 2-cm/
3/4-inch thick

4 wheat tortillas

1 avocado

2 tomatoes, thinly sliced

4 tbsp soured cream

4 spring onions,
thinly sliced

barbecued steak fajitas

To make the marinade, put the oil, lime rind and juice, garlic, coriander, cumin, sugar and salt and pepper to taste into a large, shallow, non-metallic dish large enough to hold the steak and mix together. Add the steak and turn in the marinade to coat it. Cover and leave to marinate in the refrigerator for 6–8 hours or up to 24 hours, turning occasionally.

When ready to cook, preheat the barbecue. Using a slotted spoon, remove the steak from the marinade, put on to an oiled grill rack and cook over a medium heat for 5 minutes for rare or 8–10 minutes for medium, turning the steak frequently and basting once or twice with any remaining marinade.

Meanwhile, warm the tortillas according to the instructions on the packet. Peel and slice the avocado.

Thinly slice the steak across the grain and arrange an equal quantity of the slices on one side of each tortilla. Add the tomato and avocado slices, top with a spoonful of soured cream and sprinkle over the spring onions. Fold over and eat immediately.

serves 4–6

450 g/1 lb rump steak or top-side, freshly minced

1 onion, grated

2–4 garlic cloves, crushed

2 tsp wholegrain mustard

pepper

2 tbsp olive oil

450 g/1 lb onions, finely sliced

2 tsp light muscovado sugar

hamburger buns, to serve

the classic hamburger

Place the minced steak, grated onion, garlic, mustard and pepper in a large bowl and mix together. Shape into 4–6 equal-sized burgers, then cover and leave to chill for 30 minutes.

Meanwhile, heat the oil in a heavy-based frying pan. Add the finely sliced onions and sauté over a low heat for 10–15 minutes, or until the onions have caramelized. Add the sugar after 8 minutes and stir occasionally during cooking. Drain well on kitchen paper and keep warm.

Preheat the barbecue. Cook the burgers over hot coals for 3–5 minutes on each side or until cooked to personal preference. Serve in hamburger buns with the onions.

serves 2

225 g/8 oz fillet steak, about 2.5-cm/1-inch thick

8 raw unpeeled tiger prawns

salt and pepper

4 tbsp butter

2 garlic cloves, crushed

3 tbsp chopped fresh flat-leaf parsley, plus extra parsley sprigs, to garnish

finely grated rind and juice of 1 lime

olive oil, for oiling

lime wedges, to garnish

crusty bread, to serve

surf 'n' turf skewers

Cut the steak into 2.5-cm/1-inch cubes. To prepare the prawns, use your fingers to pull off their heads, then peel off their shells, leaving the tails on. Using a sharp knife, make a shallow slit along the outside of each prawn, then pull out the dark vein and discard. Rinse the prawns under cold running water and dry well on kitchen paper.

Thread an equal number of the steak cubes and prawns on to 2 oiled metal kebab skewers or presoaked wooden skewers. Season the kebabs to taste with pepper.

Preheat the barbecue. Meanwhile, put the butter and garlic into a small saucepan and heat gently until melted. Remove from the heat and add the parsley, lime rind and juice and salt and pepper to taste. Leave in a warm place so that the butter remains melted. Brush the kebabs with a little of the melted butter. Put the kebabs on to an oiled grill rack and cook over hot coals for 4–8 minutes until the steak is cooked according to your taste and the prawns turn pink, turning the kebabs frequently during cooking, and brushing with the remaining melted butter.

Serve the kebabs hot on the skewers, with the remaining butter spooned over. Garnish with lime wedges and parsley sprigs and serve with crusty bread to mop up the buttery juices.

serves 4

4 lean pork loin chops

4 tbsp clear honey

1 tbsp dry sherry

4 tbsp orange juice

2 tbsp olive oil

2.5-cm/1-inch piece
fresh ginger, grated

sunflower oil, for oiling

salt and pepper

honey-glazed pork chops

Preheat the barbecue. Season the pork chops with salt and pepper to taste. Reserve while you make the glaze.

To make the glaze, place the honey, sherry, orange juice, olive oil and ginger in a small saucepan and heat gently, stirring constantly, until well blended.

Cook the pork chops on an oiled rack over hot coals for 5 minutes on each side.

Brush the chops with the glaze and barbecue for a further 2–4 minutes on each side, basting frequently with the glaze.

Transfer the pork chops to warmed serving plates and serve hot.

serves 4

1 onion, chopped

2 garlic cloves, chopped

2.5-cm/1-inch piece
fresh ginger, sliced

1 fresh red chilli, deseeded
and chopped

5 tbsp dark soy sauce

3 tbsp lime juice

1 tbsp palm or muscovado
sugar

2 tbsp groundnut oil

1 kg/2 lb 4 oz pork spare ribs,
separated

salt and pepper

sprigs of coriander,
to garnish

spicy ribs

Preheat the barbecue. Put the onion, garlic, ginger, chilli and soy sauce into a food processor and process to a paste. Transfer to a jug and stir in the lime juice, sugar and oil and season to taste with salt and pepper.

Place the spare ribs in a preheated wok or large, heavy-based saucepan and pour in the soy sauce mixture. Place on the hob and bring to the boil, then simmer over a low heat, stirring frequently, for 30 minutes. If the mixture appears to be drying out, add a little water.

Remove the spare ribs, reserving the sauce. Cook the ribs over medium hot coals, turning and basting frequently with the sauce, for 20–30 minutes. Transfer to a large serving plate and serve immediately, garnished with coriander.

serves 4

450 g/1 lb pork fillet

300 ml/10 fl oz dry cider

1 tbsp fresh sage

6 black peppercorns, crushed

2 crisp eating apples

1 tbsp sunflower oil

crusty bread, to serve

normandy brochettes

Using a sharp knife, cut the pork into 2.5-cm/1-inch cubes, then place in a large, shallow, non-metallic dish. Mix the cider, sage and peppercorns together in a jug, pour the mixture over the pork and turn until thoroughly coated. Cover with clingfilm and leave to marinate in the refrigerator for 1–2 hours.

Preheat the barbecue. Drain the pork, reserving the marinade. Core the apples, but do not peel, then cut into wedges. Dip the apple wedges into the reserved marinade and thread on to several metal skewers, alternating with the cubes of pork. Stir the sunflower oil into the remaining marinade.

Cook the brochettes over medium hot coals, turning and brushing frequently with the reserved marinade, for 12–15 minutes. Transfer to a large serving plate and if you prefer, remove the meat and apples from the skewers before serving. Serve immediately with crusty bread.

serves 6

6 chump chops, about
175 g/6 oz each

150 ml/5 fl oz natural Greek
yogurt

2 garlic cloves, finely
chopped

1 tsp grated fresh ginger

1/4 tsp coriander seeds,
crushed

1 tbsp olive oil, plus extra for
brushing

1 tbsp orange juice

1 tsp walnut oil

2 tbsp chopped fresh mint,
plus sprigs to garnish

salt and pepper

minted lamb chops

Place the chops in a large, shallow, non-metallic bowl. Mix half
the yogurt, the garlic, ginger and coriander seeds together in a
jug and season to taste with salt and pepper. Spoon the mixture
over the chops, turning to coat, then cover with clingfilm
and leave to marinate in the refrigerator for 2 hours, turning
occasionally.

Preheat the barbecue. Place the remaining yogurt, the olive oil,
orange juice, walnut oil and mint in a small bowl and, using
a hand-held blender, mix until thoroughly blended. Season
to taste with salt and pepper. Cover the minted yogurt with
clingfilm and leave to chill in the refrigerator until ready to
serve.

Drain the chops, scraping off the marinade. Brush with olive
oil and cook over medium hot coals for 5–7 minutes on each
side. Garnish with mint springs and serve immediately with the
minted yogurt.

serves 4

4 chicken drumsticks

4 chicken thighs

2 fresh corn cobs, husks and silks removed

85 g/3 oz butter, melted

fresh flat-leaf parsley sprigs, to garnish

spice mix

2 tsp onion powder

2 tsp paprika

1^1/$_2$ tsp salt

1 tsp garlic powder

1 tsp dried thyme

1 tsp cayenne pepper

1 tsp ground black pepper

^{1}/$_2$ tsp ground white pepper

^{1}/$_4$ tsp ground cumin

cajun chicken

Preheat the barbecue. Using a sharp knife, make 2–3 diagonal slashes in the chicken drumsticks and thighs, then place them in a large dish. Cut the corn cobs into thick slices and add them to the dish. Mix all the ingredients for the spice mix together in a small bowl.

Brush the chicken and corn with the melted butter and sprinkle with the spice mix. Toss to coat well.

Cook the chicken over medium hot coals, turning occasionally, for 15 minutes, then add the corn slices and cook, turning occasionally, for a further 10–15 minutes, or until beginning to blacken slightly at the edges. Transfer to a large serving plate and serve immediately, garnished with parsley.

serves 4

4 lean chicken portions

1 bunch spring onions, trimmed

1–2 Scotch Bonnet chillies, deseeded

1 garlic clove

5-cm/2-inch piece ginger, peeled and roughly chopped

1/2 tsp dried thyme

1/2 tsp paprika

1/4 tsp ground allspice

pinch ground cinnamon

pinch ground cloves

4 tbsp white wine vinegar

3 tbsp light soy sauce

pepper

jerk chicken

Rinse the chicken portions and pat them dry on absorbent kitchen paper. Place them in a shallow dish.

Place the spring onions, chillies, garlic, ginger, thyme, paprika, allspice, cinnamon, cloves, wine vinegar, soy sauce and pepper to taste in a food processor and process until smooth.

Pour the spicy mixture over the chicken. Turn the chicken portions over so that they are well coated in the marinade.

Transfer the chicken portions to the refrigerator and leave to marinate for up to 24 hours.

Remove the chicken from the marinade and barbecue over medium hot coals for about 30 minutes, turning the chicken over and basting occasionally with any remaining marinade, until the chicken is browned and cooked through.

Transfer the chicken portions to individual serving plates and serve immediately.

serves 4

4 large chicken breast fillets,
skinned

1 large egg white

1 tbsp cornflour

1 tbsp plain flour

1 egg, beaten

55 g/2 oz fresh white
breadcrumbs

2 tbsp sunflower oil

2 beef tomatoes, sliced

to serve

hamburger buns

lettuce

mayonnaise

the ultimate chicken burger

Place the chicken breasts between 2 sheets of non-stick baking
paper and flatten slightly using a meat mallet or a rolling pin.
Beat the egg white and cornflour together, then brush over the
chicken. Cover and leave to chill for 30 minutes, then coat in the
flour.

Place the egg and breadcrumbs in 2 separate bowls and coat the
burgers first in the egg, allowing any excess to drip back into the
bowl, then in the breadcrumbs.

Preheat the barbecue. Lightly brush each burger with a little oil
and then add them to the barbecue grill, cooking over medium
hot coals for 6–8 minutes on each side, or until thoroughly
cooked. If you are in doubt, it is worth cutting one of the burgers
in half. If there is any sign of pinkness, cook for a little longer
to get that nice barbecue taste. Add the tomato slices to the
grill rack for the last 1–2 minutes of the cooking time to heat
through. Serve the burgers in hamburger buns with the lettuce,
cooked tomato slices and mayonnaise.

serves 4

4 skinless, boneless chicken breasts, about 175 g/6 oz each

finely grated rind and juice of 1/2 lemon

finely grated rind and juice of 1/2 orange

2 tbsp clear honey

2 tbsp olive oil

2 tbsp chopped fresh mint, plus extra to garnish

1/4 tsp ground coriander

salt and pepper

citrus zest, to garnish

zesty kebabs

Using a sharp knife, cut the chicken into 2.5-cm/1-inch cubes, then place them in a large glass bowl. Place the lemon and orange rind, the lemon and orange juice, the honey, oil, mint and ground coriander in a jug and mix together. Season to taste with salt and pepper. Pour the marinade over the chicken cubes and toss until they are thoroughly coated. Cover with clingfilm and leave to marinate in the refrigerator for up to 8 hours.

Preheat the barbecue. Drain the chicken cubes, reserving the marinade. Thread the chicken on to several long metal skewers.

Cook the skewers over medium hot coals, turning and brushing frequently with the reserved marinade, for 6–10 minutes, or until thoroughly cooked. Transfer to a large serving plate, garnish with chopped mint and citrus zest and serve immediately.

Fish & Seafood

serves 4

4 salmon steaks, about
175 g/6 oz each

finely grated rind
and juice of 1 lime or
1/2 lemon

salt and pepper

lemon wedges, to serve

mango salsa

1 large mango, peeled, stoned
and diced

1 red onion, finely chopped

2 passion fruit

2 fresh basil sprigs

2 tbsp lime juice

salt

salmon with mango salsa

Preheat the barbecue. Rinse the salmon steaks under cold running water, pat dry with kitchen paper and place in a large, shallow, non-metallic dish. Sprinkle with the lime rind and pour the juice over them. Season to taste with salt and pepper, cover and leave to stand while you make the salsa.

To make the salsa, place the mango flesh in a bowl with the onion. Cut the passion fruit in half and scoop out the seeds and pulp with a teaspoon into the bowl. Tear the basil leaves and add them to the bowl with the lime juice. Season to taste with salt and stir well. Cover with clingfilm and reserve until required.

Cook the salmon steaks over medium hot coals for 3–4 minutes on each side. Serve immediately with the salsa and lemon wedges.

serves 4

4 white fish steaks

1 tbsp paprika

1 tsp dried thyme

1 tsp cayenne pepper

1 tsp black pepper

1/2 tsp white pepper

1/2 tsp salt

1/4 tsp ground allspice

50 g/1 3/4 oz unsalted butter

3 tbsp sunflower oil

green beans, to serve

charred fish

Preheat the barbecue. Rinse the fish steaks under cold running water and pat dry with kitchen paper.

Mix the paprika, thyme, cayenne, black and white peppers, salt and allspice together in a shallow dish.

Place the butter and sunflower oil in a small saucepan and heat gently, stirring occasionally, until the butter melts.

Brush the butter mixture liberally all over the fish steaks, on both sides, then dip the fish into the spicy mix until coated on both sides.

Cook the fish over hot coals for 3 minutes on each side until cooked through. Continue to baste the fish with the remaining butter mixture during the cooking time. Serve with the green beans.

chargrilled tuna with chilli sauce

serves 4

4 tuna steaks, about 175 g/6 oz each

grated rind and juice of 1 lime

2 tbsp olive oil

salt and pepper

fresh coriander sprigs, to garnish

lettuce leaves, to serve

crusty bread, to serve

chilli sauce

2 orange peppers

1 tbsp olive oil

juice of 1 lime

juice of 1 orange

2–3 fresh red chillies, deseeded and chopped

pinch of cayenne pepper

Rinse the tuna thoroughly under cold running water and pat dry with kitchen paper, then place in a large, shallow, non-metallic dish. Sprinkle with the lime rind and pour the juice and olive oil over the fish. Season to taste with salt and pepper, cover with clingfilm and leave to marinate in the refrigerator for up to 1 hour.

Preheat the barbecue. To make the sauce, brush the peppers with the olive oil and cook over hot coals, turning frequently, for 10 minutes, or until the skin is blackened and charred. Remove from the barbecue and leave to cool slightly, then peel off the skins and discard the seeds. Put the peppers into a food processor with the remaining sauce ingredients and process to a purée. Transfer to a bowl and season to taste with salt and pepper.

Cook the tuna over hot coals for 4–5 minutes on each side, until golden. Transfer to serving plates, garnish with coriander sprigs and serve with the sauce, lettuce leaves and plenty of crusty bread.

serves 4–6

225 g/8 oz sweet potatoes, chopped

450 g/1 lb fresh tuna steaks

6 spring onions, finely chopped

175 g/6 oz courgette, grated

1 fresh red jalapeño chilli, deseeded and finely chopped

2 tbsp prepared mango chutney

1 tbsp sunflower oil

salt

lettuce leaves, to serve

mango salsa

1 large ripe mango, peeled and stoned

2 ripe tomatoes, finely chopped

1 fresh red jalapeño chilli, deseeded and finely chopped

4-cm/1½-inch piece cucumber, finely diced

1 tbsp chopped fresh coriander

1–2 tsp clear honey

tuna burgers with mango salsa

Cook the sweet potatoes in a saucepan of lightly salted boiling water for 15–20 minutes, or until tender. Drain well, then mash and place in a food processor. Cut the tuna into chunks and add to the potatoes.

Add the spring onions, courgette, chilli and mango chutney to the food processor and, using the pulse button, blend together. Shape into 4–6 equal-sized burgers, then cover and leave to chill for 1 hour.

Meanwhile make the salsa. Slice the mango flesh, reserving 8–12 good slices for serving. Finely chop the remainder, then mix with the tomatoes, chilli, cucumber, coriander and honey. Mix well, then spoon into a small bowl. Cover and leave for 30 minutes to allow the flavours to develop.

Preheat the barbecue. Brush the burgers lightly with oil and cook over hot coals for 4–6 minutes on each side, or until piping hot. Serve with the mango salsa, garnished with lettuce leaves and the reserved slices of mango.

serves 4

6 spring onions

400 ml/14 fl oz coconut milk

finely grated rind and juice of 1 lime

4 tbsp chopped fresh coriander, plus extra to garnish

2 tbsp corn or sunflower oil

pepper

650 g/1 lb 7 oz raw tiger prawns

lemon wedges, to garnish

coconut prawns

To prepare the prawns, use your fingers to pull off their heads, then peel off their shells, leaving the tails on. Using a sharp knife, make a shallow slit along the outside of each prawn, then pull out the dark vein and discard. Rinse the prawns under cold running water and dry well on kitchen paper.

Finely chop the spring onions and place in a large, shallow, non-metallic dish with the coconut milk, lime rind and juice, coriander and oil. Mix well and season to taste with pepper. Add the prawns, turning to coat. Cover with clingfilm and leave to marinate in the refrigerator for 1 hour.

Preheat the barbecue. Drain the prawns, reserving the marinade. Thread the prawns on to 8 long metal skewers.

Cook the skewers over medium hot coals, brushing with the reserved marinade and turning frequently, for 8 minutes, or until they have changed colour. Serve the prawns immediately, garnished with the lemon wedges and chopped coriander.

serves 6

36 large, raw tiger prawns

2 tbsp finely chopped fresh coriander

pinch of cayenne pepper

3–4 tbsp corn oil

fresh coriander leaves, to garnish

lemon wedges, to serve

citrus sauce

1 orange

1 tart eating apple, peeled, quartered and cored

2 fresh red chillies, deseeded and chopped

1 garlic clove, chopped

8 fresh coriander sprigs

8 fresh mint sprigs

4 tbsp lime juice

salt and pepper

prawns with citrus sauce

Preheat the barbecue. To make the sauce, peel the orange and cut into segments. Reserve any juice. Put the orange segments, apple quarters, chillies, garlic, coriander and mint into a food processor and process until smooth. With the motor running, add the lime juice through the feeder tube. Transfer the sauce to a serving bowl and season to taste with salt and pepper. Cover with clingfilm and leave to chill in the refrigerator until required.

Using a sharp knife, remove and discard the heads from the prawns, then peel off the shells. Cut along the back of the prawns and remove the dark intestinal vein. Rinse the prawns under cold running water and pat dry with kitchen paper. Mix the chopped coriander, cayenne and corn oil together in a dish. Add the prawns and toss well to coat.

Cook the prawns over medium hot coals for 3 minutes on each side, or until they have changed colour. Transfer to a large serving plate, garnish with fresh coriander leaves and serve immediately with lemon wedges and the salsa.

serves 8

2 oranges

2 lemons

2 monkfish tails, about
500 g/1 lb 2 oz each, skinned
and cut into 4 fillets

8 fresh lemon thyme sprigs

2 tbsp olive oil

salt

2 tbsp green peppercorns,
lightly crushed

orange & lemon peppered monkfish

Cut 8 orange slices and 8 lemon slices, reserving the remaining fruit. Rinse the monkfish fillets under cold running water and pat dry with kitchen paper. Place the monkfish fillets, cut side up, on a work surface and divide the citrus slices among them. Top with the lemon thyme. Tie each fillet at intervals with kitchen string to secure the citrus slices and thyme. Place the monkfish in a large, shallow, non-metallic dish.

Squeeze the juice from the remaining fruit and mix with the olive oil in a jug. Season to taste with salt, then spoon the mixture over the fish. Cover with clingfilm and leave to marinate in the refrigerator for up to 1 hour, spooning the marinade over the fish tails once or twice.

Preheat the barbecue. Drain the monkfish tails, reserving the marinade. Sprinkle the crushed green peppercorns over the fish, pressing them in with your fingers. Cook the monkfish over medium hot coals, turning and brushing frequently with the reserved marinade, for 20–25 minutes. Transfer to a chopping board, remove and discard the string and cut the monkfish tails into slices. Serve immediately.

serves 6

1 kg/2 lb 4 oz swordfish steaks

3 tbsp olive oil

3 tbsp lime juice

1 garlic clove, finely chopped

1 tsp paprika

3 onions, cut into wedges

6 tomatoes, cut into wedges

salt and pepper

caribbean fish kebabs

Using a sharp knife, cut the fish into 2.5-cm/1-inch cubes and place in a shallow, non-metallic dish. Place the oil, lime juice, garlic and paprika in a jug and mix well. Season to taste with salt and pepper. Pour the marinade over the fish, turning to coat. Cover with clingfilm and leave to marinate in the refrigerator for 1 hour.

Preheat the barbecue. Thread the fish cubes, onion wedges and tomato wedges alternately on to 6 long, presoaked wooden skewers. Reserve the marinade.

Cook the kebabs over medium hot coals for 8–10 minutes, turning and brushing frequently with the reserved marinade. When they are cooked through, transfer the kebabs to a large serving plate and serve immediately.

serves 6

36 fresh oysters

18 streaky bacon rashers, rinded

1 tbsp mild paprika

1 tsp cayenne pepper

sauce

1 fresh red chilli, deseeded and finely chopped

1 garlic clove, finely chopped

1 shallot, finely chopped

2 tbsp finely chopped fresh parsley

2 tbsp lemon juice

salt and pepper

chargrilled devils

Preheat the barbecue. Open the oysters, catching the juice from the shells in a bowl. Cut the oysters from the bottom shells, reserve and tip any remaining juice into the bowl. To make the sauce, add the red chilli, garlic, shallot, parsley and lemon juice to the bowl, then season to taste with salt and pepper and mix well. Cover the bowl with clingfilm and leave to chill in the refrigerator until required.

Cut each bacon rasher in half across the centre. Season the oysters with paprika and cayenne, then roll each oyster up inside half a bacon rasher. Thread 6 wrapped oysters on to each of the 6 presoaked wooden skewers.

Cook over hot coals, turning frequently, for 5 minutes, or until the bacon is well browned and crispy. Transfer to a large serving plate and serve immediately with the sauce.

Vegetarian & Accompaniments

serves 4–6

85 g/3 oz brown rice

400 g/14 oz canned flageolet beans, drained

115 g/4 oz unsalted cashew nuts

3 garlic cloves

1 red onion, cut into wedges

115 g/4 oz sweetcorn kernels

2 tbsp tomato purée

1 tbsp chopped fresh oregano

2 tbsp wholemeal flour

2 tbsp sunflower oil

salt and pepper

to serve

hamburger buns

lettuce leaves

tomato slices

cheese slices

the ultimate vegetarian burger

Preheat the barbecue. Cook the rice in a saucepan of lightly salted boiling water for 20 minutes, or until tender. Drain and place in a food processor.

Add the beans, cashew nuts, garlic, onion, sweetcorn, tomato purée, oregano and salt and pepper to the rice in the food processor and, using the pulse button, blend together. Shape into 4–6 equal-sized burgers, then coat in the flour. Cover and leave to chill for 1 hour.

Lightly brush the burgers with oil. When the barbecue is hot, cook the burgers over medium hot coals for 5–6 minutes on each side or until cooked and piping hot. Serve the burgers in hamburger buns with the salad leaves, and tomato and cheese slices.

serves 4

350 g/12 oz firm tofu

1 red pepper

1 yellow pepper

2 courgettes

8 button mushrooms

marinade

grated rind and
juice of 1/2 lemon

1 garlic clove, crushed

1/2 tsp chopped fresh
rosemary

1/2 tsp chopped fresh thyme

1 tbsp walnut oil

to garnish

shredded carrot

lemon wedges

marinated tofu skewers

To make the marinade, mix the lemon rind and juice, garlic, rosemary, thyme and walnut oil together in a shallow dish. Drain the tofu, pat it dry on kitchen paper and cut it into squares. Add to the marinade and toss to coat. Leave to marinate for 20–30 minutes.

Preheat the barbecue. Deseed the peppers and cut into 2.5-cm/ 1-inch pieces. Blanch in boiling water for 4 minutes, refresh in cold water and drain. Using a canelle knife or potato peeler, remove strips of peel from the courgettes. Cut the courgettes into 2.5-cm/1-inch chunks.

Remove the tofu from the marinade, reserving the liquid for basting. Thread the tofu on to 8 presoaked wooden skewers, alternating with the peppers, courgette and button mushrooms.

Cook the skewers over medium hot coals for 6 minutes, turning and basting with the marinade. Transfer the skewers to warmed serving plates, garnish with shredded carrot and lemon wedges and serve.

serves 2

1 small bunch of
fresh mint

2 large courgettes

1 tbsp olive oil, plus extra for
brushing

115 g/4 oz feta cheese,
cut into strips

pepper

courgette & cheese parcels

Preheat the barbecue. Using a sharp knife, finely chop
enough mint to fill 1 tablespoon. Reserve until required. Cut
out 2 rectangles of foil, each large enough to enclose a courgette,
and brush lightly with olive oil. Cut a few slits along the length
of each courgette and place them on the foil rectangles.

Insert strips of feta cheese along the slits in the courgettes,
then drizzle the olive oil over the top, sprinkle with the reserved
chopped mint and season to taste with pepper. Fold in the sides
of the foil rectangles securely and seal the edges to enclose the
cheese-stuffed courgettes completely.

Bake the courgette parcels in the barbecue embers for 30–40
minutes. Carefully unwrap the parcels and serve immediately.

serves 4

1 tbsp olive oil

2 tbsp pine kernels

1 onion, finely chopped

1 garlic clove, finely chopped

500 g/1 lb 2 oz fresh spinach, thick stalks removed and leaves shredded

pinch of freshly grated nutmeg

4 beef tomatoes

140 g/5 oz mozzarella cheese, diced

salt and pepper

stuffed tomato parcels

Preheat the barbecue. Heat the oil in a heavy-based saucepan. Add the pine kernels and cook, stirring constantly, for 2 minutes, or until golden. Add the onion and cook over a low heat, stirring occasionally, for 5 minutes, or until softened but not browned. Add the garlic and spinach, cover and cook for 2–3 minutes, or until the spinach has wilted. Remove the saucepan from the heat and season to taste with nutmeg, salt and pepper. Leave to cool.

Using a sharp knife, cut off and reserve a thin slice from the top of each tomato and scoop out the flesh with a teaspoon, taking care not to pierce the shell. Chop the flesh and stir it into the spinach mixture with the mozzarella cheese.

Fill the tomato shells with the spinach and cheese mixture and replace the tops. Cut 4 squares of foil, each large enough to enclose a tomato. Place one tomato in the centre of each square and fold up the sides to enclose securely. Cook over hot coals, turning occasionally, for 10 minutes. Serve immediately in the foil parcels.

serves 12

12 open-cap mushrooms

4 tsp olive oil

4 spring onions, chopped

100 g/3¹/₂ oz fresh brown breadcrumbs

1 tsp chopped fresh oregano

100 g/3¹/₂ oz feta cheese or chorizo sausage

sunflower oil, for oiling

stuffed mushrooms

Preheat the barbecue. Remove the stalks from the mushrooms and chop the stalks finely. Heat half of the olive oil in a large frying pan. Add the mushroom stalks and spring onions and sauté briefly.

Mix the mushroom stalks and spring onions together in a large bowl. Add the breadcrumbs and oregano to the mushrooms and spring onions, mix well, then reserve until required.

If using feta, crumble the cheese into small pieces in a small bowl. If you are using chorizo sausage, remove the skin and chop the flesh finely.

Add the crumbled feta cheese or chopped chorizo to the breadcrumb mixture and mix well. Spoon the stuffing mixture into the mushroom caps.

Drizzle the remaining olive oil over the stuffed mushrooms, then cook on an oiled rack over medium hot coals for 8–10 minutes. Transfer the mushrooms to individual serving plates and serve while still hot.

serves 4

1 red onion

1 fennel bulb

4 baby aubergines

4 baby courgettes

1 orange pepper

1 red pepper

2 beef tomatoes

2 tbsp olive oil

salt and pepper

1 fresh basil sprig,
to garnish

creamy pesto

55 g/2 oz fresh basil leaves

15 g/1/2 oz pine kernels

1 garlic clove

pinch of coarse sea salt

25 g/1 oz freshly grated
Parmesan cheese

50 ml/2 fl oz extra virgin
olive oil

150 ml/5 fl oz natural Greek
yogurt

chargrilled vegetables with creamy pesto

Preheat the barbecue. To make the pesto, place the basil, pine kernels, garlic and sea salt in a mortar and pound to a paste with a pestle. Gradually work in the Parmesan cheese, then gradually stir in the oil.

Place the yogurt in a small serving bowl and stir in 3–4 tablespoons of the pesto mixture. Cover with clingfilm and leave to chill in the refrigerator until required. Store any leftover pesto mixture in a screw-top jar in the refrigerator.

Prepare the vegetables. Cut the onion and fennel bulb into wedges, trim and slice the aubergines and courgettes, deseed and thickly slice the peppers and cut the tomatoes in half. Brush the vegetables with oil and season to taste with salt and pepper.

Cook the aubergines and peppers over hot coals for 3 minutes, then add the courgettes, onion, fennel and tomatoes and cook, turning occasionally and brushing with more oil if necessary, for a further 5 minutes. Transfer to a large serving plate and serve immediately with the pesto, garnished with a basil sprig.

serves 4

225 g/8 oz dried fusilli

4 tomatoes

50 g/1¾ oz black olives

25 g/1 oz sun-dried tomatoes
in oil

2 tbsp freshly grated
Parmesan cheese

2 tbsp pine kernels

salt and pepper

fresh basil leaves,
to garnish

basil vinaigrette

15 g/½ oz basil leaves

1 garlic clove, crushed

2 tbsp freshly grated
Parmesan cheese

4 tbsp extra virgin olive oil

2 tbsp lemon juice

pasta salad with basil vinaigrette

Cook the pasta in a large saucepan of lightly salted boiling water for 10–12 minutes, or until just tender but still firm to the bite. Drain the pasta, rinse under cold running water, then drain again thoroughly. Place the pasta in a large bowl.

Preheat the grill to medium. To make the vinaigrette, place the basil leaves, garlic, cheese, olive oil and lemon juice in a food processor. Season to taste with salt and pepper and process until the leaves are well chopped and the ingredients are combined. Alternatively, finely chop the basil leaves by hand and combine with the other vinaigrette ingredients. Pour the vinaigrette over the pasta and toss to coat.

Cut the tomatoes into wedges. Stone and halve the olives. Slice the sun-dried tomatoes. Toast the pine kernels on a baking tray under the hot grill until golden.

Add the tomatoes (fresh and sun-dried) and the olives to the pasta and mix until combined.

Transfer the pasta to a serving dish, sprinkle over the Parmesan and toasted pine kernels and serve garnished with a few basil leaves.

serves 4

350 g/12 oz green beans, trimmed

1 red onion, chopped

3–4 tbsp chopped fresh coriander

2 radishes, thinly sliced

75 g/2¾ oz feta cheese, crumbled

1 tsp chopped fresh oregano or ½ tsp dried oregano

pepper

2 tbsp red wine or fruit vinegar

5 tbsp extra virgin olive oil

6 ripe cherry or small tomatoes, quartered

green bean & feta salad

Bring about 5 cm/2 inches of water to the boil in the base of a steamer or in a medium saucepan. Add the green beans to the top of the steamer or place them in a metal colander set over the pan of water. Cover and steam for about 5 minutes until just tender.

Transfer the beans to a bowl and add the onion, coriander, radishes and feta cheese.

Sprinkle the oregano over the salad, then grind pepper over to taste. Whisk the vinegar and olive oil together and then pour over the salad. Toss gently to mix well.

Transfer to a serving platter, surround with the tomato quarters and serve at once or chill until ready to serve.

serves 4

700 g/1 lb 9 oz tiny new potatoes

8 spring onions

1 hard-boiled egg (optional)

250 ml/9 fl oz mayonnaise

1 tsp paprika

salt and pepper

to garnish

2 tbsp snipped fresh chives

pinch of paprika

potato salad

Bring a large saucepan of lightly salted water to the boil. Add the potatoes and cook for 10–15 minutes, or until they are just tender.

Drain the potatoes and rinse them under cold running water until completely cold. Drain again. Transfer the potatoes to a bowl and reserve until required. Using a sharp knife, slice the spring onions thinly on the diagonal. Chop the hard-boiled egg, if using.

Mix the mayonnaise, paprika and salt and pepper to taste together in a bowl. Pour the mixture over the potatoes. Add the spring onions and egg, if using, to the potatoes and toss together.

Transfer the potato salad to a serving bowl, sprinkle with snipped chives and a pinch of paprika. Cover and leave to chill in the refrigerator until required.

serves 4–6

8 small baking potatoes, scrubbed

50 g/1³/4 oz butter, melted

salt and pepper

optional topping

6 spring onions, sliced

50 g/1³/4 oz grated Gruyère cheese

50 g/1³/4 oz salami, cut into thin strips

crispy potato skins

Preheat the oven to 200°C/400°F/Gas Mark 6. Prick the potatoes with a fork and bake for 1 hour, or until tender. Alternatively, cook in a microwave on High for 12–15 minutes. Cut the potatoes in half and scoop out the flesh, leaving about 5 mm/¹/4 inch potato flesh lining the skin.

Preheat the barbecue. Brush the insides of the potato with melted butter.

Place the skins, cut-side down, over medium hot coals and cook for 10–15 minutes. Turn the potato skins over and barbecue for a further 5 minutes, or until they are crispy. Take care that they do not burn. Season the potato skins with salt and pepper to taste and serve while they are still warm.

If wished, the skins can be filled with a variety of toppings. Barbecue the potato skins as above for 10 minutes, then turn cut-side up and sprinkle with slices of spring onion, grated cheese and chopped salami. Barbecue for a further 5 minutes, or until the cheese begins to melt. Serve hot.

serves 6

150 g/5^1/$_2$ oz butter, softened

3 cloves garlic, crushed

2 tbsp chopped fresh parsley

pepper

1 large or 2 small sticks of French bread

garlic bread

Mix together the butter, garlic and parsley in a bowl until well combined. Season with pepper to taste and mix well.

Cut a few lengthways slits in the French bread. Spread the flavoured butter inside the slits and place the bread on a large sheet of thick kitchen foil.

Preheat the barbecue. Wrap the bread well in the foil and barbecue over hot coals for 10–15 minutes until the butter melts and the bread is piping hot.

Serve as an accompaniment to a wide range of dishes.

Desserts & Treats

serves 4

2 dessert apples, cored and
cut into wedges

2 firm pears, cored and
cut into wedges

juice of 1/2 lemon

25 g/1 oz light muscovado
sugar

1/4 tsp ground allspice

25 g/1 oz unsalted butter,
melted

toffee sauce

125 g/41/2 oz butter

100 g/31/2 oz light muscovado
sugar

6 tbsp double cream

toffee fruit kebabs

Preheat the barbecue. Toss the apples and pears in the lemon juice to prevent
any discoloration.

Mix the sugar and allspice together and sprinkle over the fruit. Thread the
fruit pieces on to skewers.

To make the sauce, place the butter and sugar in a saucepan and heat,
stirring gently, until the butter has melted and the sugar has dissolved.

Add the cream to the saucepan and bring to the boil. Boil for
1–2 minutes, then leave to cool slightly.

Meanwhile, place the fruit kebabs over hot coals and cook for
5 minutes, turning and basting frequently with the melted butter, until the
fruit is just tender. Transfer the fruit kebabs to warmed serving plates and
serve with the cooled toffee sauce.

serves 4

1 tbsp butter, softened

225 g/8 oz plain or milk chocolate

4 large bananas

2 tbsp rum

crème fraîche, mascarpone cheese or ice cream, to serve

grated nutmeg, to decorate

chocolate rum bananas

Take four 25-cm/10-inch squares of aluminium foil and brush them with butter.

Grate the chocolate. Make a careful slit lengthways in the peel of each banana, and open just wide enough to insert the chocolate. Place the grated chocolate inside the bananas, along their lengths, then close them up.

Wrap each stuffed banana in a square of foil, then barbecue them over hot coals for about 5–10 minutes, or until the chocolate has melted inside the bananas. Remove from the barbecue, place the bananas on individual serving plates and pour some rum into each banana.

Serve immediately with crème fraîche, mascarpone cheese or ice cream, topped with nutmeg.

serves 4

4 peaches

175 g/6 oz mascarpone
cheese

40 g/1 1/2 oz pecan nuts or
walnuts, chopped

1 tsp sunflower oil

4 tbsp maple syrup

mascarpone peaches

Cut the peaches in half and remove the stones. If you are preparing this recipe in advance, press the peach halves together and wrap in clingfilm until required.

Mix the mascarpone cheese and pecans together in a bowl until well combined. Leave to chill in the refrigerator until required. Preheat the barbecue. Brush the peach halves with a little sunflower oil and place on a rack set over medium hot coals. Cook the peach halves for 5–10 minutes, turning once, until hot.

Transfer the peach halves to a serving dish and top with the mascarpone and nut mixture. Drizzle the maple syrup over the peaches and mascarpone filling and serve immediately.

serves 4

1 pineapple

3 tbsp dark rum

2 tbsp muscovado sugar

1 tsp ground ginger

4 tbsp unsalted butter, melted

totally tropical pineapple

Preheat the barbecue. Using a sharp knife, cut off the crown of the pineapple, then cut the fruit into 2-cm/³⁄₄-inch thick slices. Cut away the peel from each slice and flick out the 'eyes' with the point of the knife. Stamp out the cores with an apple corer or small pastry cutter.

Mix the rum, sugar, ginger and butter together in a jug, stirring constantly, until the sugar has dissolved. Brush the pineapple rings with the rum mixture.

Cook the pineapple rings over hot coals for 3–4 minutes on each side. Transfer to serving plates and serve immediately with the remaining rum mixture poured over them.

serves 4

8 fresh figs

100 g/3¹/₂ oz cream cheese

1 tsp powdered cinnamon

3 tbsp brown sugar

natural yogurt, crème fraîche, mascarpone cheese or ice cream, to serve

stuffed figs

Cut out eight 18-cm/7-inch squares of aluminium foil. Make a small slit in each fig, then place each fig on a square of foil.

Put the cream cheese in a bowl. Add the cinnamon and stir until well combined. Stuff the inside of each fig with the cinnamon cream cheese, then sprinkle a teaspoon of sugar over each one. Close the foil round each fig to make a parcel.

Place the parcels on the barbecue and cook over hot coals, turning them frequently, for about 10 minutes, or until the figs are cooked to your taste.

Transfer the figs to serving plates and serve immediately with natural yogurt, crème fraîche, mascarpone cheese or ice cream.

serves 4

225 g/8 oz strawberries

25 g/1 oz caster sugar

6 tbsp Marsala wine

$^1/_2$ tsp ground cinnamon

4 slices panettone

4 tbsp mascarpone cheese

panettone with mascarpone & strawberries

Hull and slice the strawberries and place them in a bowl. Add the sugar, Marsala and cinnamon to the strawberries.

Toss the strawberries in the sugar and cinnamon mixture until they are well coated. Leave to chill in the refrigerator for at least 30 minutes. Preheat the barbecue. When ready to serve, transfer the slices of panettone to a rack set over medium hot coals. Cook the panettone for 1 minute on each side, or until golden brown.

Remove the panettone from the barbecue and transfer to serving plates. Top the panettone with the mascarpone cheese and the marinated strawberries. Serve immediately.

serves 4

2 nectarines, halved and stoned

2 kiwi fruit

4 red plums

1 mango, peeled, halved and stoned

2 bananas, peeled and thickly sliced

8 strawberries, hulled

1 tbsp clear honey

3 tbsp Cointreau

mixed fruit kebabs

Cut the nectarine halves into wedges and place in a large, shallow dish. Peel and quarter the kiwi fruit. Cut the plums in half and remove the stones. Cut the mango flesh into chunks and add to the dish with the kiwi fruit, plums, bananas and strawberries.

Mix the honey and Cointreau together in a jug until well blended. Pour the mixture over the fruit and toss lightly to coat. Cover with clingfilm and leave to marinate in the refrigerator for 1 hour.

Preheat the barbecue. Drain the fruit, reserving the marinade. Thread the fruit on to several presoaked wooden skewers and cook over medium hot coals, turning and brushing frequently with the reserved marinade, for 5–7 minutes, then serve.

makes 2 litres/3¹/2 pints

1.5 litres/2³/4 pints red grape juice

300 ml/10 fl oz orange juice

75 ml/2¹/2 fl oz cranberry juice

50 ml/1³/4 fl oz lemon juice

50 ml/1³/4 fl oz lime juice

100 ml/3¹/2 fl oz sugar syrup

ice cubes

to decorate

slices of lemon

slices of orange

slices of lime

soft sangria

Put the grape juice, orange juice, cranberry juice, lemon juice, lime juice and sugar syrup into a chilled punch bowl and stir well.

Add the ice and decorate with the slices of lemon, orange and lime.

apples
  Normandy brochettes 22
  prawns with citrus sauce 47
  toffee fruit kebabs 80
aubergines: chargrilled vegetables with creamy pesto 67
avocados: barbecued steak fajitas 13

bacon: chargrilled devils 52
bananas
  chocolate rum bananas 83
  mixed fruit kebabs 92
beans: ultimate vegetarian burger 56
beef
  barbecued steak fajitas 13
  brandy steaks 11
  classic hamburger 14
  surf 'n' turf skewers 17
bread
  garlic bread 76
  panettone with mascarpone & strawberries 91
burgers
  classic hamburger 14
  tuna burgers with mango salsa 43
  ultimate chicken burger 30
  ultimate vegetarian burger 56

cheese
  chargrilled vegetables with creamy pesto 67
  courgettes and cheese parcels 60
  crispy potato skins 75
  green bean and feta salad 71
  pasta salad with basil vinaigrette 68
  stuffed mushrooms 64
  stuffed tomato parcels 63
  see also cream cheese
chicken
  Cajun chicken 26
  jerk chicken 29
  ultimate chicken burger 30
  zesty kebabs 33
chillies
  chargrilled devils 52
  chargrilled tuna with chilli sauce 40
  jerk chicken 29
  prawns with citrus sauce 47
  spicy ribs 21
  tuna burgers with mango salsa 43
chocolate rum bananas 83
chorizo: stuffed mushrooms 64
coconut prawns 44
courgettes
  chargrilled vegetables with creamy pesto 67
  courgettes and cheese parcels 60
  marinated tofu skewers 59
  tuna burgers with mango salsa 43
cream cheese
  mascarpone peaches 84
  panettone with mascarpone & strawberries 91
  stuffed figs 88

fennel: chargrilled vegetables with creamy pesto 67
figs: stuffed figs 88
fish & seafood
  Caribbean fish kebabs 51
  chargrilled devils 52
  chargrilled tuna with chilli sauce 40
  charred fish 39
  coconut prawns 44
  orange & lemon peppered monkfish 48
  prawns with citrus sauce 47
  salmon with mango salsa 36
  tuna burgers with mango salsa 43
fruit
  chocolate rum bananas 83
  mascarpone peaches 84
  mixed fruit kebabs 92

Normandy brochettes 22
panettone with mascarpone & strawberries 91
prawns with citrus sauce 47
salmon with mango salsa 36
stuffed figs 88
toffee fruit kebabs 80
totally tropical pineapple 87
tuna burgers with mango salsa 43
see also lemons; limes; oranges

garlic bread 76
ginger
  honey-glazed pork chops 18
  jerk chicken 29
  minted lamb chops 25
  spicy ribs 21
  totally tropical pineapple 87
green bean and feta salad 71

honey
  honey-glazed pork chops 18
  mixed fruit kebabs 92
  tuna burgers with mango salsa 43
  zesty kebabs 33

kebabs
  Caribbean fish kebabs 51
  marinated tofu skewers 59
  mixed fruit kebabs 92
  surf 'n' turf skewers 17
  toffee fruit kebabs 80
  zesty kebabs 33
kiwi fruit: mixed fruit kebabs 92

lamb: minted lamb chops 25
lemons
  marinated tofu skewers 59
  orange & lemon peppered monkfish 48
  salmon with mango salsa 36
  soft sangria 95
  zesty kebabs 33
limes
  barbecued steak fajitas 13
  Caribbean fish kebabs 51
  chargrilled tuna with chilli sauce 40
  coconut prawns 44
  prawns with citrus sauce 47
  salmon with mango salsa 36
  soft sangria 95
  spicy ribs 21
  surf 'n' turf skewers 17

mangoes
  mixed fruit kebabs 92
  salmon with mango salsa 36
  tuna burgers with mango salsa 43
monkfish: orange & lemon peppered monkfish 48
mushrooms
  marinated tofu skewers 59
  stuffed mushrooms 64

nectarines: mixed fruit kebabs 92
nuts
  mascarpone peaches 84
  ultimate vegetarian burger 56

onions & spring onions
  barbecued steak fajitas 13
  Caribbean fish kebabs 51
  chargrilled vegetables with creamy pesto 67
  classic hamburger 14
  coconut prawns 44
  crispy potato skins 75
  green bean and feta salad 71
  jerk chicken 29
  potato salad 72

salmon with mango salsa 36
stuffed mushrooms 64
tuna burgers with mango salsa 43
ultimate vegetarian burger 56
oranges
  chargrilled tuna with chilli sauce 40
  honey-glazed pork chops 18
  orange & lemon peppered monkfish 48
  prawns with citrus sauce 47
  soft sangria 95
  zesty kebabs 33
oysters: chargrilled devils 52

passion fruit: salmon with mango salsa 36
pasta salad with basil vinaigrette 68
peaches: mascarpone peaches 84
pears: toffee fruit kebabs 80
peppers
  chargrilled tuna with chilli sauce 40
  chargrilled vegetables with creamy pesto 67
  marinated tofu skewers 59
pine kernels
  chargrilled vegetables with creamy pesto 67
  pasta salad with basil vinaigrette 68
  stuffed tomato parcels 63
pineapple: totally tropical pineapple 87
plums: mixed fruit kebabs 92
pork
  honey-glazed pork chops 18
  Normandy brochettes 22
  spicy ribs 21
potatoes
  crispy potato skins 75
  potato salad 72
prawns
  coconut prawns 44
  prawns with citrus sauce 47
  surf 'n' turf skewers 17

radishes: green bean and feta salad 71
rice: ultimate vegetarian burger 56

salads
  green bean and feta salad 71
  pasta salad with basil vinaigrette 68
  potato salad 72
salami: crispy potato skins 75
salmon with mango salsa 36
soft sangria 95
spinach: stuffed tomato parcels 63
strawberries
  mixed fruit kebabs 92
  panettone with mascarpone & strawberries 91
sweet potatoes: tuna burgers with mango salsa 43
sweetcorn
  Cajun chicken 26
  ultimate vegetarian burger 56
swordfish: Caribbean fish kebabs 51

toffee fruit kebabs 80
tofu: marinated tofu skewers 59
tomatoes
  barbecued steak fajitas 13
  Caribbean fish kebabs 51
  chargrilled vegetables with creamy pesto 67
  green bean and feta salad 71
  pasta salad with basil vinaigrette 68
  stuffed tomato parcels 63
  tuna burgers with mango salsa 43
  ultimate chicken burger 30
tuna
  chargrilled tuna with chilli sauce 40
  tuna burgers with mango salsa 43

yogurt
  chargrilled vegetables with creamy pesto 67